JASON CLARKSON

ROGER ST. HAMMOND

JAMES STEED

BBC Children's Books
Published by the Penguin Group
Penguin Books Ltd, 80 Strand, London, WC2R 0RL, England
Penguin Group (Australia) Ltd, 250 Camberwell Road, Camberwell, Victoria 3124, Australia (a division of Pearson Australia Group Pty Ltd)
Canada, India, New Zealand, South Africa

Published by BBC Children's Books, 2012
Text and design © Children's Character Books, 2012

001 – 10 9 8 7 6 5 4 3 2 1

Written by Dan Newman
USA Road Trip Challenge written by Kevin Pettman and illustrated by Kevin Hopgood

ISBN: 9781405908450

Printed in Italy

Picture credits: P15 – Smart Fortwo: LovelaceMedia/Shutterstock.com. P21 – E-Type: Bocman1973/Shutterstock.com, old Fiat 500 & old
VW Beetle: Joost J. Bakker, new Fiat 500: Mauritsvink, MG TF & new Mini Cooper: The_Car_Spy, old Mini Cooper: Sicnag, new & old VW
Scirocco: Rudolf Stricker. P27 – yellow Porsche 911: Pat Durkin. Page 29 – Lewis Hamilton: Jaggat, top right & bottom left: David Acosta
Allely, pit crew: Chen Wei Seng, wheel: Faiz Zaki, champagne: Natursports (All Shutterstock.com). P57 Ferrari 365 GTB-4 & Jaguar XK120:
Brian Snelson, Ferrari F40: Spezadams, Mercedes 300SL: Andrew Basterfield.

TopGear Annual 2013

Contents

Introduction

Hello and welcome! What have been the highs and lows this year for Jeremy, James, Richard and The Stig?

'This is a **brilliant, brilliant, brilliant** car. And that's all, really, I've got to say. **The end.**'
(BMW 1M)

'I think this, by a long way, is the most **beautiful car** I've ever **seen**. It might actually be the most **beautiful thing** I've ever seen.'
(Eagle Speedster)

'Oh my God! What an **extraordinary day!** What a **fantastic** moment.'

'This is quite **horrible.** I don't like this. **No, no, no.** I don't want this.'

'I don't think I've ever been in a car that has **launched itself** quite like that!'
(Nissan GT-R)

Jeremy

'The **ride** in this **is excellent.** Mrs Beckham, I have to **commend** you on **your car.**'

'Bang! Oh yes!'
(Mini WRC)

'Look at this! It's a train, and it works! Ha ha! This is just the best thing I've ever done!'

'Urgh! Aargh! Woorgh! Aah!'

'It **could have been** a **comfortable** gentlemen's express. Instead it's just another **pointless bone-shaking** racing **car.**'

James

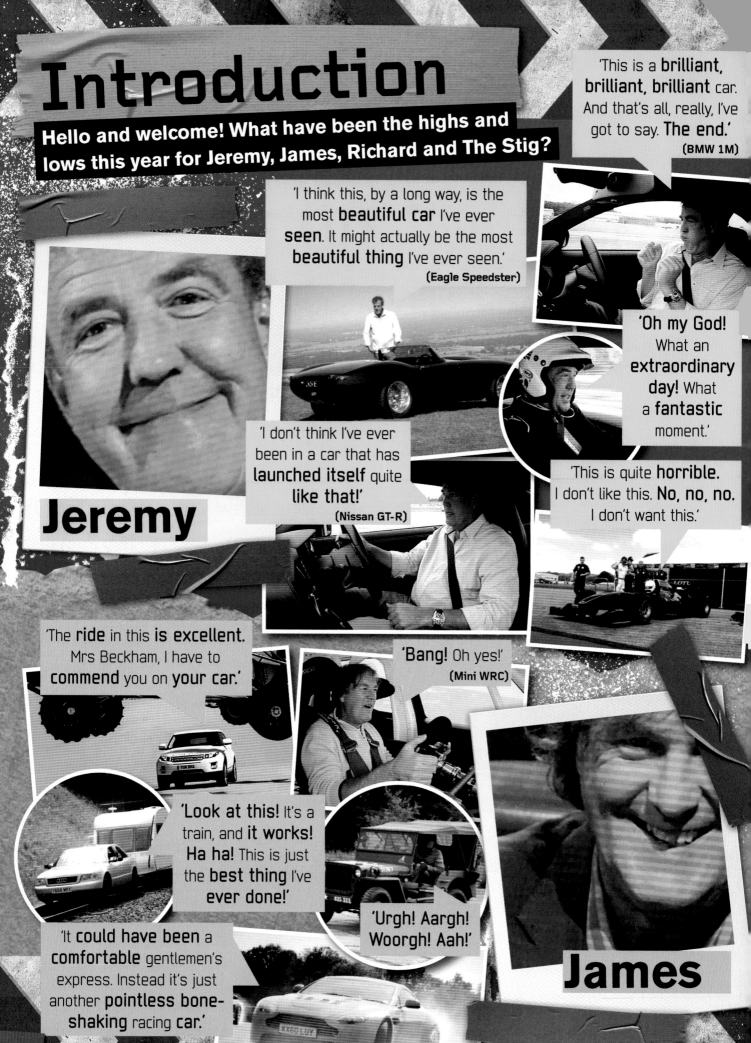

Richard

'It's really kind of the ideal **shopping car!**'

'What makes this car better than Jeremy's is . . . **pop-up headlamps!**'

'That's **absolutely brutal!** It kicks **you** in the **back** of the **head!**'
(Lamborghini Aventador)

'Ha haaa! We need one of these!'

'**Wow,** that could be a **castle** . . . or a **den** . . . or a **car** . . . I've **never** thrown a shoebox away.'

1.17.8s
Nissan GT-R

1.03.8s
Lotus T125

1.16.5s
Lambo Aventador

1.16.2s
McLaren MP4-12C

The Stig

1.25.0s
BMW 1M

1.24.4s
Aston Martin Virage

'Stay Away from India!'

That's what the Prime Minister said to Jeremy, Richard and James. For some reason, they decided to ignore him.

THE PLAN

Take some second-hand British cars (costing under £7000) to India and show off how brilliant they are, to persuade India to buy more stuff from us.

THE CARS

JAMES

Series 1 Rolls-Royce Silver Shadow from 1976. Handmade in Crewe by Brits, not like modern Rollers.

'It is her Majesty the Queen, with a tax disc. And **lovely carpet.**'

JEREMY

Jaguar XJ-S, Celebration model, with a 4-litre straight-six engine and a poor reputation.

'The engine is **smooth**, all the **electrics work** . . . this is a mobile advertisement for **Great Britain**. Never mind that **Jag today is Indian.**'

RICHARD

Mini Cooper Sport from 2000 in lovely condition.

'Ha haa! This is the **perfect car** for this place. It is a puppy, yes, but it's a **Staffordshire Bull Terrier.** A tough little puppy.'

THE ROUTE

Start from Mumbai and drive 1,300 dangerous miles through Jaipur, Delhi, Shimla and into Kashmir in the Himalayas.

! The Emergency Back-up Car
A white Austin Allegro. Don't break down, chaps!

shimla
deli
jaipur
india
mumbai

Race the Bombay dabbawallahs from the suburbs to the centre. These chaps take 200,000 home-cooked hot lunches to office workers every day with amazing efficiency. Jeremy reckoned using cars rather than trains could improve this already brilliant service. He raced off on time, but left loads of lunches behind, which Richard had to load on his little roof. James was left behind, trying to sort out the fiddly codes. Jeremy made it first, and just beat the train, but only delivered sixteen lunches. Richard lost loads of lunches

FAIL!

whipping round a corner, got stuck in traffic and was badly late. James headed for the ring road . . . and got lost.

Catch the train to Jaipur. While James queued to buy the tickets, Jeremy and Richard bought some musical instruments. Then while trying to hang banners on the train promoting Britain, James managed to get left behind. And the banners ripped.

BRITISH IT FOR YOUR COMPANY

THE UNITED KINGDOM PROMOTES

FAIL!

Promote the British motor-racing industry with The Top Gear All India Classic British Hill Climb Event. Many Indian vehicles competed, including a Rajdoot 175 motorbike (1.20.6), a Hindustani Ambassador (1.23.4), a Tata Nano (1.14.7) and an elephant (32.00). Richard stormed up, but deliberately held back so as not to show up their hosts (1.17.2). James was also thoughtful and considerate (1.19.6). Jeremy did what he always does, and won.

FAIL!

Decorate the cars in Indian style. James went for an elephant theme, Jeremy fitted wallpaper racing stripes and an outside loo, and Richard attempted to paint the Indian flag on his bonnet – but actually did the Mexican flag. Whoops.

Host a swanky party in Delhi to impress some influential locals. James crashed a lawnmower through a window, Jeremy crashed a JCB into the Roller and took off his trousers, Richard got the guests' car keys mixed up. The *Top Gear* band was pretty unimpressive, too.

FAIL!

FAIL!

'Oh God! I've ruined everything. It's no use trying to say anything intelligent to you, **it's just too noisy.**'

Upgrade your cars to cope with the rough roads to come. Richard didn't do much to the Mini, sensibly. Jeremy and James ruined their cars with huge tyres and cranked-up suspension. So the rides were awful. And the noise!

Head into the Himalayas. The mountains were beautiful, but the roads were shocking and there weren't many chances to sell British products. Richard turned his Mini into a clown car after ripping the bonnet off trying to winch James up a slope. They ended up camping, which made Jeremy grumpy. But the cars, amazingly, made it to the top of the world.

'These 3 fantastic cars have been **better** ambassadors for Britain than we could ever be.'

WIN!

'Powerrr!'

FAIL!

Complete the Quote

Can you guess which ridiculous phrase the boys used to describe these cars? Fill in the blanks with your silliest suggestion . . . then find out what they actually said!

Answers on page 60

'The 1M is like a _____ _____. It's made of leftovers.'

BMW 1M

Eagle Speedster

'It's spitting fire . . . it's a _____! That's what it is!'

McLaren MP4-12C

'You'd get more of a jolt if you drove a Rolls-Royce over a _____.'

'The McLaren, then, is like a _____. Very practical, and very sensible.'

'It's like off-roading in a _____!'

Marauder

'This is not a car, it's a _____.'

Ferrari 599 GTO

Range Rover Evoque

'Lovely, lovely tarmac. It's like a _____ _____.'

'It feels and sounds as if it's being fuelled by a mixture of plutonium and _____.'

'Everyone should own a _____ at some point or you are incomplete as a human being.'

Jaguar XKR-S

Colour-me Stig

Get your pens out and fill in this pic of The Stig, using his favourite colours. Each section is numbered – use the guide to work out which colour to use where.

Colour guide
1 Milk
2 Snow
3 Cotton
4 Santa's beard
5 Wedding dress
6 Teeth
7 Mashed potato
8 Cloud
9 White

When Big Jezza was Little

Ever wondered why Jeremy loves cars so much? Let's take a look at the things he grew up with as a child.

Supercar costing £2098

Supermodel

Skateboard

Games console

MP3 player

Laptop computer

Mobile phone

The Internet

Plasma TV

Half a Kilo of Motorcar, Please

The Marauder that Richard drove weighs almost ten tons. How many cars could you balance on the other side of a really big set of scales?

Marauder

- ⏱ **0-60mph:** who knows?
- 🚗 **Power:** 300hp
- ⏲ **Top speed:** 75mph

> The Marauder can carry ten soldiers with all their kit, plus machine guns and missile launchers. It can keep going for over 400 miles and is tough enough to withstand being blown up by 14kg of TNT. No wonder it's heavy!

300kg

RoadRazer
- ⏱ **0-60mph:** 3.0s
- 🚗 **Power:** 180hp
- ⏲ **Top speed:** 150mph

440kg

Westfield Megabusa
- ⏱ **0-60mph:** 3.25s
- 🚗 **Power:** 175hp
- ⏲ **Top speed:** 130mph

450kg

Radical SR4
- ⏱ **0-60mph:** 3.5s
- 🚗 **Power:** 210hp
- ⏲ **Top speed:** 145mph

450kg

Caterham R500
- ⏱ **0-60mph:** 2.95s
- 🚗 **Power:** 263hp
- ⏲ **Top speed:** 150mph

470kg

Caparo T1
- ⏱ **0-60mph:** 2.55s
- 🚗 **Power:** 575hp
- ⏲ **Top speed:** 205mph

876kg

Lotus Elise
- 0–60mph: 6.05s
- Power: 134hp
- Top speed: 126mph

864kg

Chevrolet Matiz
- 0–60mph: 15.55s
- Power: 68hp
- Top speed: 96mph

840kg

Fiat Panda
- 0–60mph: 15.05s
- Power: 54hp
- Top speed: 93mph

800kg

Peugeot 107
- 0–60mph: 13.75s
- Power: 68hp
- Top speed: 98mph

9,900kg

795kg

Smart Fortwo
- 0–60mph: 8.95s
- Power: 85hp
- Top speed: 90mph

790kg

Toyota Aygo
- 0–60mph: 14.25s
- Power: 67hp
- Top speed: 98mph

540kg

Ariel Atom
- 0–60mph: 2.35s
- Power: 487hp
- Top speed: 175mph

700kg

Morgan 4/4
- 0–60mph: 9.85s
- Power: 95hp
- Top speed: 100mph

790kg

KTM X-Bow
- 0–60mph: 3.95s
- Power: 237hp
- Top speed: 135mph

790kg

Citroën C1
- 0–60mph: 13.35s
- Power: 68hp
- Top speed: 98mph

Multiple Choice Marauder

Could you drive a Marauder? Take the Top Gear Official Marauder Driving Test* to find out if you're capable of taming this monster!

1) **You are driving your Marauder down a quiet country road when you find your route blocked by a fallen tree. Do you:**

   a   Stop your vehicle and call the emergency services

   b   Attempt to clear the tree from the road yourself

   c   Drive straight over it and carry on

2) **You are driving down a road when you reach a narrow section where someone has parked a Morris Marina. There isn't enough room for you to get past. Do you:**

   a   Sound your horn to call the Marina driver back, and ask them to move

   b   Carefully turn your Marauder round and find another route

   c   Drive straight over the Marina and carry on

3) **You are driving your Marauder after heavy rain and find the road has flooded ahead of you. The water is almost a metre deep. Do you:**

   a   Stop your vehicle and call the emergency services

   b   Go home and wait

   c   Drive straight through the water and carry on

4) **After leaving your Marauder for a few days near a building site, you come back to find a large brick wall has been built around it. Do you:**

   a   Go and complain to the foreman and get the wall taken down

   b   Contact your insurers and get them to sort it out

   c   Drive straight through the wall and carry on

5) **You are driving your Marauder down the High Street when an earthquake suddenly hits and the earth splits open in front of you. There's an 80cm crack (with lava at the bottom) across the road. Do you:**

   a   Stop, get out of the Marauder and run away

   b   Wait for the earth to stop moving and then see what you can do to help

   c   Drive straight over the crack and carry on

* Not official

16

6) After getting slightly lost on the way to see your Gran, you find yourself on the wrong side of a mountain. Do you:

a   Call Gran and say you're not going to make it   ☐

b   Get there as fast as you can and apologise   ☐

c   Drive straight over the mountain and carry on to Gran's   ☐

7) After getting rather lost again, you find yourself in a desert – 400 miles from anywhere. Do you:

a   Cry and panic   ☐

b   Wait calmly for someone to rescue you   ☐

c   Drive straight out of the desert and carry on   ☐

8) After getting extremely lost, you find yourself in a minefield. Do you:

a   Cry and panic   ☐

b   Reverse out very, very slowly   ☐

c   Drive straight over the mines and carry on   ☐

'There was a **fight** between the **Marauder** and the Earth. And **the Earth lost.**'

Scoring

0 for every time you answered **a**

2 for every time you answered **b**

10 for every time you answered **c**

How did you do?

60–80:   You clearly already own a Marauder. Congratulations, and remember to be careful when going to a drive-through restaurant.

20–59:   With practice, you could be a Marauder driver. Why not try out the correct techniques in your current vehicle? **(WARNING: DO NOT ATTEMPT TO DRIVE ANY OTHER CAR AS IF IT WAS A MARAUDER.)**

0–20:   You are never going to be a Marauder driver. To be honest, the only way you'll get near one is if it drives over you.

In Case You Missed It

It's been a busy year in TG Land. Here's a quick reminder of what the chaps got up to.

'It's like **Monaco** in many ways, actually. Have you ever been to **Hammersmith?**'

'**Look!** Leather, **leather-**leather-leather, **wood,** leather, leather-leather. **Leather,** leather, **leather.**'

Richard liked one word a lot.

James went for a little drive.

'**Hang on,** now I'm **going** the **wrong way.**'

'It won't start.'

19

James' Orienteering Challenge

Can you follow James' instructions and get out of town? Which exit will you end up at?

'Right . . . no, **not right**, er, **straight** on. **North**, I think. Yes, North. When the road opens out into a square, **head East**.
'Take **the third** – no, **second right**. It's at another square, bigger than the last one but not as big as the one you started in.
'**Carry on forwards** as much as you can, it's a bit **wiggly**. Take the . . . **fourth right**, go around the bend and forwards until – ah. Umm . . . take the **next exit** out of the square **on your left**. Take the **second right**, then the next left. Wind your way towards the edge of town. Then go around the town **clockwise** until you find an **exit**.'

'Is that it? What, just drive out of town? Well, **how hard can that be?**'

A

B

N
W · E
S

F

Start

E

C

Answer on page 60

D

'This **must be James's** idea of hell. He **gets lost** in a **hotel**.'

20

Modern Classics

Car manufacturers love to make modern versions of old classics. Can you match the new car to its historic inspiration? And can you name them?

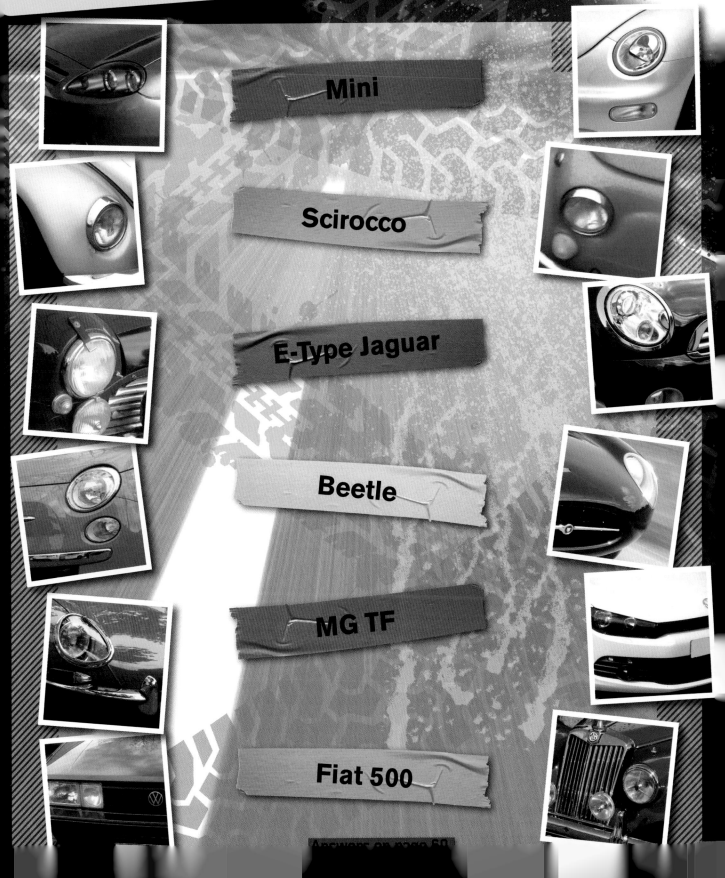

Mini

Scirocco

E-Type Jaguar

Beetle

MG TF

Fiat 500

Answers on page 59

How to Name a Car

Thinking up a name for a car is easy. Giving a car a GOOD name, however . . .

A lot of the good names have already been used, so carmakers use numbers more these days, or made-up words that won't upset anyone in countries where they want to sell cars. Here are a few genuine car names from around the world – see if your opinion matches ours. Remember – this is just about the *name*, not about the car they're attached to!

	GOOD	BAD
Animals	Barracuda, Bronco, Cobra, Colt, Cougar, Eagle, Hornet, Jaguar, Mustang, Panther, Phoenix, Ram, Raptor, Stag, Wildcat, Viper	Beetle, Impala, Kitten, Panda, Pony, Rabbit, Spider, Super Bee, Tercel (a hawk)
Things	Arrow, Corvette (a small warship), Cutlass, Dart, Javelin, Legend, Lightning, Magnum, Mirage, Patrol, Phantom, Prairie, Rodeo, Safari, Scimitar, Scirocco (an Italian wind), Sierra, Silver Cloud, Spirit, Star Chief, Storm, Zonda (an Argentine wind)	Avalanche, Belvedere, Blazer, Bongo, Breeze, Brougham, Charade, Citation, Contour, Coronet, Corolla, Cube, Domino, Duster, Echo, Edge, Essence, Medallion, Metro, Midget, Prelude, Passport, Probe, Pulsar, Quintet, Scamp, Silhouette, Sonata, Stylus, Sunbeam, Visa
Jobs	Aviator, Brigand, Cavalier, Champ, Corsair, Explorer, Highlander, Hunter, Marquis, Matador, Navigator, Pathfinder, Pilot, Warlock, Wrangler	Ambassador, Celebrity, Cooper, Courier, Diplomat, Envoy, Executive, Fairlady, Forester, Graduate, Princess, Sidekick, Starlet, Villager
Actions and Sports	Avenger, Challenger, Charger, Conquest, Fury, Interceptor, Intrepid, Lancer, Marauder, Rally, Rampage, Range Rover, Sprint, Stealth	Acclaim, Accord, Ascender, Aspire, Civic, Cruiser, Escort, Excel, Focus, Golf, Growler, Hummer, Intrigue, Polo, Prowler, Quest, Samba, Sunny, Swinger
Names and Places	Capri, Colorado, Cortina, Eldorado, Le Mans, Malibu, Monaco, Monte Carlo, Outback, Rio, Riviera, Seville	Aston Martin Cygnet and Colette, Calais, Cherry, Cressida, Dolomite, Justy, Somerset, Sonoma, Suburban, Tahoe, Versailles, Yukon
Foreign	Carrera (race) Comanche (stranger), Diablo (devil), Élan (spirit), Esprit (spirit again), Fuego (fire), Mystique (mysterious), Quattro (four), Shogun (general), Virage (curve), Volante (flying), Volare (fly)	Alero (soft ground), Allegro (lively), Eclat (brilliant), Estoque (sword), Protégé (protected one), Sigma (S), Stanza (stopping place), Strada (road), Testarossa (redhead), Viva (live)
Made-up	Arnage, Bravada, Sportage	Altima, Aztek, Camry, Celica, Chevette, Econoline, Elantra, Integra, Leganza, LeSabre, Lumina, Luv, Nubira, Prizm, Reatta, Sebring, Tercel, Tredia, Xantia, Xterra

What's your car name?

Choose the first part from your first initial and the second part from your last initial:

Initial	First part	Second part
A	Anaconda	Architect
B	Boomerang	Bureaucrat
C	Condor	Capacious
D	Dachsund	Dictator
E	Exocet	Eloquent
F	Ferret	Facilitator
G	Grizzly	Genteel
H	Harpoon	Hasty
I	Ibex	Ingenious
J	Jackrabbit	Jeroboam
K	Kestrel	Kinetic
L	Lemming	Leader
M	Mastodon	Magic
N	Nighthawk	Nimble
O	Otter	Overlord
P	Pike	Punctual
Q	Quirt	Quartermaster
R	Ramrod	Reliable
S	Stiletto	Supervisor
T	Terrier	Tyrant
U	Ungulate	Ubiquitous
V	Viking	Vagrant
W	Whirlwind	Workaholic
X	Xiphoid	Xenophile
Y	Yak	Yeoman
Z	Zebra	Zippy

Unpronounceable?
Pagani Huayra (Hruhurr)
SSC Tuatara (Twutowrr)
VW Touareg (Tow-rag)
Lamborghini Countach (Cowntack)

'Are car makers **naming** their **cars** after the **noises** people make when they're **punched in the stomach**? Lamborghini Bleurgh.'

'It still has **the best name** ever put on a car: **Interceptor**.'

Challenger!

'It's called the **Marauder**, which is quite a **scary-sounding** name. Buttercup wouldn't sound quite right.'

And the award for the worst name goes to the ...

Daihatsu Naked

And the best name? According to Jeremy, it's the **Hammerhead i-Eagle Thrust**. Yes, Jeremy. Of course it is.

Allegro?

Naked?

69-69

Top Gear Driving Apps

Top Gear *has gone all hi-tech. Check out the latest ways* Top Gear *can help the modern motoringist!*

Air Freshener
If you like the look of a little tree swinging, but hate the smell of pine, this is perfect for you.

£0.69 BUY APP

Angry Jeremies
Hurl the little shouty heads at the Cool Wall and see where they stick! Listen to them grumble and moan!

£1.99 BUY APP

Talking Stig
Tickle his tummy, scratch his head and spin him round. Talk at him and hear Stig repeat your words back in his own special way (complete silence). Comes with a variety of outfits (white) and musical instruments (which he will stare at).

£5.99 BUY APP

Caravan Ninja
Slice through *TG*'s least-favourite mobile leisure accommodation with a variety of really big hitty things. Do well and unlock secret campsites and new weapons. Do badly and you might slice open the toilet . . .

£0.99 BUY APP

RobinReliantLogger
Every time you see one of the three-wheeled death traps (Jeremy's opinion), activate this app to warn other road users of its location.

FREE APP

Find My Pasty
When you put down your pastry-based snack, press the buttons to remind you where you left it and how warm it was. NB: does not work with kebabs or burgers.

£0.69 BUY APP

Cartris
Turn, squash and fold an enormous Jeremy so he can be squeezed into a tiny car without banging his head or doing his neck in. Then try to fit in a Great Dane and a man playing a tuba.

£0.69 BUY APP

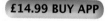

PocketJames
Instantly find out the compression ratios, camshaft duration and torque band profiles for every car ever made – plus many, many, many other really detailed facts.

£14.99 BUY APP

Morgan Run
Help a little Richard sprint round a racetrack towards a car from the last century made of wood. Keep him energized by feeding him crisps and chocolate.

£0.99 BUY APP

How Many Batteries does a Leaf Need?

8,640 AA batteries should get a Leaf 100 miles, which is enough to power . . .

a tumble dryer for six hours

a microwave for sixteen hours

a stereo for two weeks

a TV for five days

a laptop for three weeks

Blackpool Illuminations for 75 seconds

Know Your 911s

There's an all-new Porsche 911 out. The problem is, it looks exactly the same as all the old ones. Here's how to tell the different generations of 911 apart.

Pick your flavour

Every generation of 911 came in *lots* of varieties, which might include:

- **Cabriolet** – with a folding cloth roof
- **Targa** – with a removable hard roof
- **GT2 and GT3** – racing spec: more powerful, lighter and faster than normal
- **Turbo** – with, er, a turbo. Also wider, with fat wheels and a great big spoiler on the back, maybe with air intakes in front of the back wheels
- **RS** – short for rennsport, German for race sport. Lighter, less frills, bigger engine
- **CS** – Club Sport. Lighter, less frills, etc.
- **Carrera** – Spanish for race. Porsche did rather well in a Mexican race in the 1950s called the Carrera Panamericana, and uses the name on several cars.

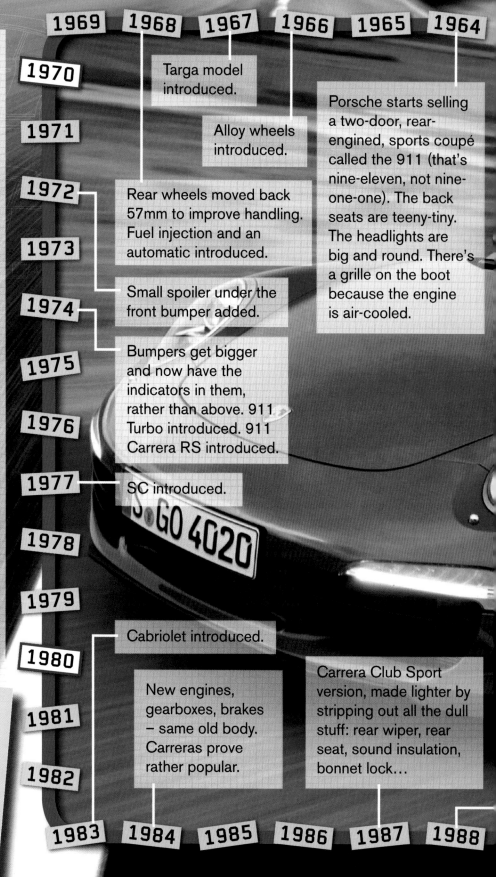

1969 1968 1967 1966 1965 1964
1970 1971 1972 1973 1974 1975 1976 1977 1978 1979 1980 1981 1982
1983 1984 1985 1986 1987 1988

Targa model introduced.

Alloy wheels introduced.

Porsche starts selling a two-door, rear-engined, sports coupé called the 911 (that's nine-eleven, not nine-one-one). The back seats are teeny-tiny. The headlights are big and round. There's a grille on the boot because the engine is air-cooled.

Rear wheels moved back 57mm to improve handling. Fuel injection and an automatic introduced.

Small spoiler under the front bumper added.

Bumpers get bigger and now have the indicators in them, rather than above. 911 Turbo introduced. 911 Carrera RS introduced.

SC introduced.

Cabriolet introduced.

New engines, gearboxes, brakes – same old body. Carreras prove rather popular.

Carrera Club Sport version, made lighter by stripping out all the dull stuff: rear wiper, rear seat, sound insulation, bonnet lock…

911 (1967)
911 (1976)
Turbo (1988)
GT2 (1995)
Turbo (2003)
Carrera 2 (2009)
Carrera S (2012)

2008

1977

2011

2010

1964

REDESIGN. Gets a bit lower, longer and wider. The wheels are now nearer the front and back. Squinty rear lights on a squarer boot. Largely made of aluminium, to save weight. Lots of other new gizmos inside.

2009

2008

2007

2006

2005

REDESIGN. Gets oval headlights back.

2004

GT3 version introduced.

2003

REDESIGN. Simpler, smoother but a bit blobby. Tear-shaped headlights borrowed from another Porsche, the Boxster. Engines are now water-cooled, which means air-intakes in the front spoiler.

2002

2001

2000

REDESIGN. Even bigger bumpers, rear end blunter, headlights less bulgy, bonnet not as low compared to the front wings. A spoiler pops up out of the back when you go fast. Speedster introduced – a low-roof version of the Cabriolet.

REDESIGN. Bonnet and wings much smoother. Headlights more oval and tipped further back from the front.

Twin-turbo version introduced.

1999

1998

1989   1990   1991   1992   1993   1994   1995   1996   1997

Monaco F1

Jeremy, James and Richard had an absolute blast in Monaco, driving the F1 Grand Prix course before the race started. What's so great about Monaco?

What is it?

Tiny: 1.98km². Only the Vatican City is smaller.

Packed: 36,000 people live there, and another 40,000 come daily to work.

Car-mad: For every thousand people, there are 863 cars.

Royal: Prince Albert II is in charge. His family, the Grimaldis, have ruled since 1297.

Peaceful: The 255 soldiers are also the firemen and policemen.

Rich: It has more millionaires and billionaires than anywhere else.

Course length 3.34km
Lap record 1m 14.4s

How come it's so rich?

Over a hundred years ago they opened a casino and a railway line to France. Rich and famous visitors loved the scenery, the climate and the gambling. Then Monaco decided it wouldn't charge any tax if they chose to live there. Now it makes more money per person than anywhere else in the world.

Is it any good as a track?

Oh yes. The course is narrow and twisty, with hills and a big tunnel. You can't see where you're going, there are loads of distractions around the track and the noise is incredible. There are faster Grand Prix tracks, but none as difficult. F1 drivers say a win here is worth two anywhere else. No wonder the chaps got so excited!

How the heck do they fit a racetrack in?

By using the normal roads. It takes six weeks to convert Monaco into one big track, and three weeks afterwards to get it back to normal. The Monaco Grand Prix has been one of the most important races in the world for over fifty years.

'I am **out of my depth** here.'

'I have to say, that's **pretty special**.'

'I can see why racing drivers **love** this track!'

Could You be an F1 Driver?

It sounds like a dream job – get paid pots of money to drive really fast in glamorous places. But have you got what it takes?

Nerves of steel
You have to go much faster than feels sensible, just to keep the downforce working – if you go any slower you'll skid.

Shoulders like a gorilla
Driving an F1 car is hard work. Drivers sweat and struggle for hours, so they need to be fit and strong.

Eyes like a hawk
You need to watch the road, the wheel, the mirrors, the cars in front, beside and behind you. All at the same time.

A neck of stone
F1 cars can go round corners incredibly fast. But that speed round the bends puts a lot of strain on your neck – your head will feel five times heavier than normal.

Handy with a bottle
It's a racing tradition that winners spray champagne over the crowd, other drivers and themselves. But those bottles are heavy, and there's a knack to getting a good spurt of fizz.

Hips like a snake
There are no fat F1 drivers. A beer belly won't fit in that tiny cockpit – even if it did, carrying spare weight would make your car slower.

A good speaking voice
When you give an interview, 500 million people may be watching. So you don't want to be squeaky. And races take place all over the world, so a talent for languages wouldn't hurt either.

Brain like a computer
Look at that wheel. You've got to work out what it's telling you, instantly. And working out what to do with all the prize money takes some brainpower, too.

Feet like a gazelle
Small, and very quick on the pedals.

The 'Bentley Mulsanne'

Jeremy was terribly disappointed with the 'Bentley Mulsanne' he took to Albania. Alright, it was actually a knackered old Yugo ... but in many ways, it was exactly the same as a brand-new Bentley.

'What the **hell** were **Bentley thinking?** Even by Albanian standards, it's **absolute rubbish.'**

Bodywork
Less of the carbon fibre, more of the medium density fibreboard. This model comes with a variety of unique dings, dents, holes, scratches and rust patches that make the Yugo such an interesting car to look at. And you can play Join the Dots on it.

Engine
Yes, it's got one. It's front-engined, like the Bentley ... though maybe not *quite* as powerful. Or as reliable, quiet, or efficient. But it can be mended in five minutes with a hammer and some WD-40.

Steering wheel
This is in the traditional posh Bentley position of 'in-front-of-one-of-the-seats'. Made of poor-quality plastic, lovingly finished by machine.

'This has to be the **least-refined** car I have **ever driven**. This is simply **intolerable**.'

Suspension
The Bentley Mulsanne has a ride smoother than polished silk. The Yugo has a ride like a giant cheese grater made of rocks.

Doors
Four of them, which make a noise when you shut them. Maybe not a dull, aristocratic 'whhummp' – in fact, more of a creaky, tinny, 'clack'.

Seats
Four of them. Not actually made of top-quality leather from happy pampered cows, but with a very strong animal smell about them. Goats? Is that goats?

Storage
There are little pockets in the door – just like the Bentley – and a glovebox and a boot. Unlike most Bentleys, this particular car seems to have been used to carry a lot of chickens and compost. Those stains won't come out in a hurry.

Wheels
Again, exactly the same number as a Bentley Mulsanne. And in similar positions – one in each corner. This has been extensively tested and proved to be the best layout (are you listening, Reliant Robin?).

Hole in the side for putting petrol in
With a locking petrol cap, to stop gangsters sucking out your valuable fuel.

Bentley Mulsanne: the facts
- **Price:** £220,000
- **Weight:** 2.8 tons
- **Engine:** twin-turbo 6.75L V8
- **Power:** 505hp
- **0–60mph:** 5.1s
- **Top speed:** 184mph

Later that day...
Jeremy catches up

WELCOME TO INDIANAPOLIS

LONG, STRAIGHT, QUIET ROADS – THIS IS THE PERFECT CAR!

HOWDY HAMSTER! LET'S WIPE THAT SMILE OFF MAY'S FACE!

WAIT UNTIL WE GET TO THE TRACK... AND STOP SAYING HOWDY !

OUR NEXT CHALLENGE IS TO COMPETE IN THE INDIANA 500!

IT'S 200 LAPS OF THE OVAL TRACK! HOW HARD CAN THAT BE?

CHALLENGE

200 LAPS? I FEEL DIZZY ALREADY!

199 laps later...

YOUR MUSCLE CAR IS PUNY, HAMMOND!

OH DO SHUT UP – YOU'RE DRIVING ME ROUND THE BEND !

OH BOTHER I'VE GOT A PUNCTURE – TIME TO RE-TYRE!

But Jeremy's beaten to the finish line!

WHAT?! IT'S THE STIG'S AMERICAN COUSIN!

BIG STIG... NO WAY !

33

The Stig Sandwich

Some say that what is inside The Stig's helmet is an absolute mystery, but with this ingenious recipe from the *Top Gear* kitchens, you can fill it with whatever takes your fancy – and then eat him.

1. First thing to do is make your favourite type of sandwich using two slices of the bread and the filling of your choice. Richard recommends a nice plain cheese or ham (no mayo, mustard, pickle, chutney or other flavouring of any kind), but you might want something more exciting . . .

Ingredients
3 slices of white bread (no bits)
Your favourite sandwich filling
Cucumber

2. Next you need to cut the sandwich into the shape of the helmet, which is squarer at the top and more rounded at the bottom.

3. If you know any sensible grown-ups, ask them to use a sharp knife to cut a large area of skin from a cucumber. Scrape off any flesh underneath it, so you are left with a flat piece of dark green skin.

38

4. Shape this piece of cucumber skin to match The Stig's visor. This is a rectangle with curved edges and an inverted V-shape for the nose area.

SOME SAY IF YOU LICK HIS CHEST, IT TASTES LIKE PICCALILLI . . .

5. To finish off the helmet, cut some thin strips of cucumber skin and put them in place for the vents.

6. The body is cut from the third slice of bread. Following the picture opposite, cut out a simple outline of the body. Highlight the arms by lightly cutting into the slice of bread but not all the way through. You can then press down on the chest with the back of a knife to define the arms.

SOME SAY HE INVENTED BRANSTON PICKLE . . .

7. Bend up the bottom of the legs to create two feet. Enjoy!

Build the Perfect Top Gear Car!

Jeremy, James and Richard are often asked which is their favourite car but, annoyingly, they keep changing their minds. There is a definitive answer though – cars which are made out of all their favourites! But can you work out what they are?

JAMES

RICHARD

LAND ROVER

RCC 127

JEREMY

Electric Car Charging Maze

Your challenge: get from the seaside to home without running out of juice. What's the best route home without having to get a push?

START

KX11 ANP

+1

+1

+1

-2

-2

Recharge

42

How to play

- This is a one-player game. Which probably helps your chances of winning.

- Your electric car can drive twenty squares before it needs to be recharged. So you start with a charge of twenty, which goes down by one for every square you land on.

- If you land on a square with a number, adjust your charge. These squares are where you're going too fast . . . or coasting downhill!

- You can't drive through lakes or woods, or across rivers or railway lines except where there's a bridge. You can't move diagonally, either.

- If your power is getting low, you **have** to get to a green recharging point before it runs out, to get filled back up to twenty 'squares' of power.

- Recharging takes all night, so don't finish the maze until, err, tomorrow!

+1

Recharge

+1

+1

-2

+1

FINISH

43

Stupid Extras

Most cars come with a base model, which is often a bit, well, basic. Not 'only three wheels and a roof made of paper' basic, but probably no satnav or alloys. You're meant to be tempted by the various 'packages' of extras that can be added.

Not these, though. These are just stupid.

£10,000

Brakes
Ceramic brakes on a Lamborghini Gallardo: £10,000 (though it's £600 cheaper if you don't want them painted). It's not as if your car doesn't come with brakes already.

Paint
Matte black paint on a Lamborghini Gallardo: £17,000. This looks cool, if you like stealth bombers. But you can't polish it, or use a car wash, or touch it.
'Liquid metal' paint on a Bentley Continental GT: £22,000.
Just a white stripe on a Ferrari 599 GTO: £7,600.

Parcel shelf
A leather parcel shelf over the engine on a Ferrari 458 Italia: £1,700.
And if you want coloured seatbelts too: £800.

£1,700

Car key
A spy-type car key for your Aston Martin Rapide, hidden in a Jaeger-LeCoultre watch: £21,000.

Spares
Spare wheel on a Ferrari California: £850 (and it's a skinny one, not a proper wheel).
Car jack ('hydraulic lifting system') on a Zonda: £9,000.

£6,000

BANG & OLUFSEN

Entertainment
Bang and Olufsen sound system with oval pop-up speakers in an Audi: £6,000 (above).
Drinks cabinet in a Rolls-Royce Phantom: £11,500.
DVD screens in a Maybach: £22,500.

What?
Chrome-painted air vents on a Porsche 911 Turbo: £550.
Flying B mascot on a Bentley: £2,000.
Ski rack on a Koenigsegg Agera: £17,000 (below).
Armour plating on a Maybach 62: £152,000. Though if you need this, then price is probably not an issue.

£17,000

Don't want to fork out for extras? Buy a Veyron. Yes it's quite expensive, but the price you pay includes all the customisation you want to get the exact car of your dreams. Now that's a bargain . . . kind of.

£1.5M

Supercars from Around the World

A lot of ambitious carmakers around the world want a slice of the valuable Veyron pie. Here's a bunch of the latest hopefuls – but can you guess which country each one is from?

Beck LM 800

Some normally-quite-sensible mountain-dwellers announced this white wedge of pricey lunacy in 2007. Since then it's all gone a bit quiet.

- **Price:** £305,000
- **Top speed:** 218mph
- **0-60mph:** 2.9s
- **Engine:** twin-turbo Audi V8
- **Power:** 1000hp

Hulme F1 Champion 1967

Named after their country's only F1 champion, this prototype impressed Aussie *Top Gear* when they drove it. It went down a storm at Goodwood. But more money is needed before real cars can be built.

- **Price:** £350,000
- **Top speed:** Have a guess
- **0-60mph:** Who knows?
- **Engine:** BMW V8
- **Power:** 560hp

Marussia B2

This was shown at the Frankfurt Motor Show in 2009. It's not that clear if they've actually made any more since then. Marussia has got involved in the Virgin F1 team, so maybe they got distracted.

- **Price:** £85,000
- **Top speed:** 160mph
- **0-60mph:** 2.7s
- **Engine:** 4.8L twin turbo
- **Power:** 1000hp

Countries to choose from:

Brazil
Canada
Finland
France
New Zealand
Poland
Russia
Switzerland

Genty Akylone

This car doesn't actually exist yet. These are computer-generated dreams. If enough people believe the dream, there may be fifteen real cars on sale in 2013.

- **Price:** who knows
- **Top speed:** 220mph
- **0-60mph:** 2.7s
- **Engine:** 4.8L twin turbo
- **Power:** 1000hp

Rossin-Bertin Vorax

A GM designer and a South American car-mad millionaire are hoping to get this built any day now. Good luck, chaps. Those performance figures are just guesses, by the way.

- **Price:** £445,000
- **Top speed:** 205mph
- **0-60mph:** 3.8s
- **Engine:** BMW supercharged V10
- **Power:** 750hp

De Veno Arrinera

It may look like a Lambo that's been kicked in the butt, but it's actually designed by the bloke that did the Ascari. Let's see if they manage to actually make some.

- **Price:** £100,000
- **Top speed:** 211mph
- **0-60mph:** 3.2s
- **Engine:** 6.2L supercharged V8
- **Power:** 638hp

HTT Pléthore LC-750

Thanks to a bit of help from the local Dragon's Den, they might start making six or seven of these a year. There are three seats, with the driver in the middle – like the McLaren F1. Cool.

- **Price:** £500,000
- **Top speed:** 240mph
- **0-60mph:** 2.8s
- **Engine:** supercharged V8
- **Power:** 750hp

Fisker Karma

Those numbers may look low for a supercar, but this is a hybrid – the petrol engine runs a generator that powers the motors. This car is actually being made, and Leonardo DiCaprio has bought one. James loves this car.

- **Price:** £85,000
- **Top speed:** 125mph
- **0-60mph:** 5.9s
- **Engine:** two 201.5hp electric motors

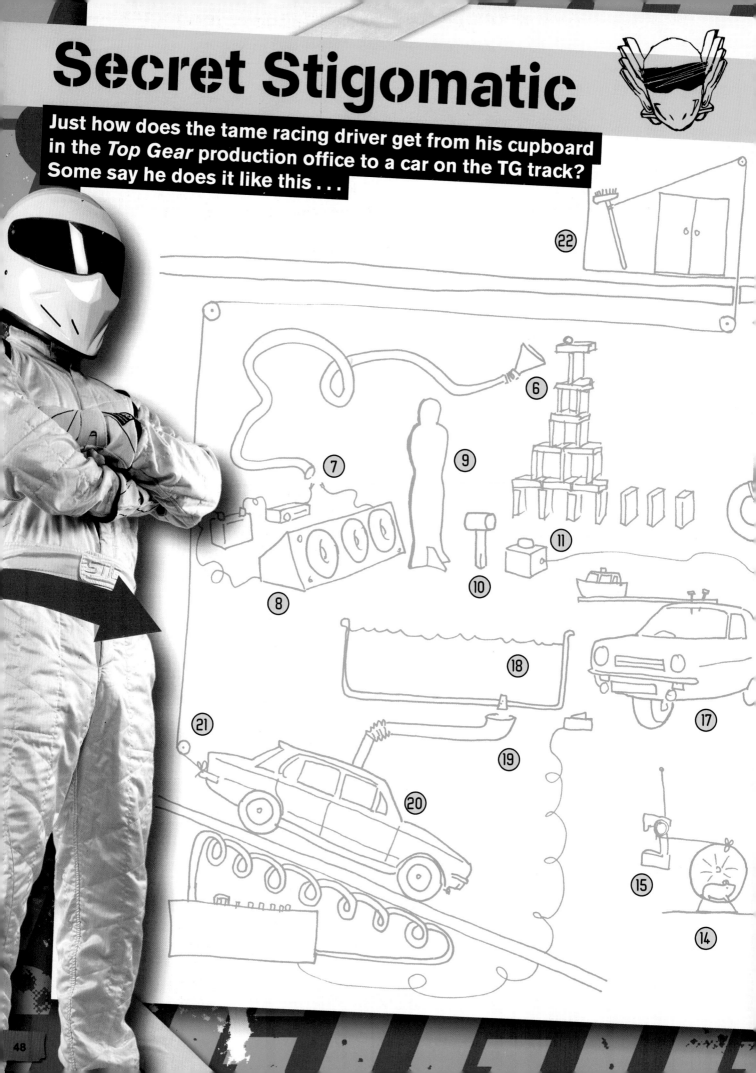

Secret Stigomatic

Just how does the tame racing driver get from his cupboard in the *Top Gear* production office to a car on the TG track? Some say he does it like this . . .

48

1. Car for testing is parked in Stig's Special Space, pressing down on manhole cover and pushing wedge down
2. Wedge dislodges golf ball, which rolls into a titanium gearwheel
3. Gearwheel falls into a black racing helmet, making it slightly heavier
4. Falling helmet lifts saw which cuts through string holding back a worn-out tyre
5. Tyre swings into other worn-out tyres, knocking into tower of old compilation videos
6. Falling videos dislodge metal ball bearing, which drops into a funnel fixed to a pipe
7. At the end of the pipe, ball bearing lodges between two wires, completing an electrical circuit and turning on the stereo taken from a dusty Mazda MX5
8. Stereo starts playing old rock music at top volume
9. Shockwave of sound knocks over life-size cardboard cut-out of Kristin Scott Thomas
10. Kristin knocks over large hammer marked 'Jeremy's Toolkit'
11. Hammer presses big red button on detonator
12. Detonator sets off tiny explosive charge, lighting gas under a full chip pan in caravan
13. Caravan catches fire and burns away, making it lighter. Morris Marina tips into pit, dragging flaming wreckage with it
14. Sound of impact wakes hamster, which starts running in wheel
15. Wheel turns, pulling on string which squeezes throttle on remote control
16. Remote control car speeds up ramp, flies through air and taps lightly on side of Reliant Robin
17. Robin tips over, dislodging toy boat made by Richard before pressing switch that turns on freezer mechanism
18. Toy boat launches into water tank and sinks instantly
19. Boat knocks out cork in bottom of tank, draining water into old British car
20. Water floods out of old British car and freezes
21. Old British car slides on ice and pulls on string, dislodging broom in *Top Gear* Production Office
22. Broom taps on Stig's cupboard, alerting The Stig who walks out to drive the car

Coppers' Cars

In the old days, American TV cops had to have a great car. But which was best? Rate them out of five stars!

Charlie's Angels *1976-81*

Sabrina Duncan, Kelley Garrett and Jill Munroe become glamorous private investigators after leaving the police. They often worked undercover, and always looked great. Remade as films more recently.

Ford Mustang Cobra II with a stripe

★★★★★

Miami Vice *1984-89*

Sonny Crockett and Ricardo Tubbs are cool undercover cops in Florida. A stylish show with great visuals and music.

Ferrari Testarossa (white in the show – all real cars were red or black).

★★★★★

Magnum PI *1980-88*

Thomas Magnum is a tough private investigator in Hawaii. He hangs out with women in bikinis, lives in some rich bloke's house and gets to use his car.

Ferrari 308 GTS

★★★★★

Hawaii 5-0 *1968-80*

Steve McGarrett is a tough cop in Hawaii. They updated this series recently.

Loads of Fords and Mercurys, including a Mercury Park Lane Brougham

★★★★★

Kojak *1973-78*

Theodopolous Kojak is a tough New York cop. He's Greek, he sucks lollipops, he's bald, he says 'Who loves ya, baby!'

Brown Buick Century Regal 455

★★★★★

Rockford Files *1974-80*

Jim Rockford is a private investigator in Los Angeles. He's been in prison, he lives in a mobile home, he's a bit shabby . . . he knows how to do a J-turn in a car.

Gold Pontiac Firebird Esprit

★★★★★

Starsky and Hutch *1975-79*

David Starsky and Ken Hutchinson are tough California cops. Remade as a comedy film in 2004.

Ford Gran Torino

★★★★★

Meanwhile, back in Britain . . .

Jeremy reminisced about the great cars on British detective shows from the 60s and 70s. He even made up a show about one of them.

The Baron: Jensen CV-8 Mk II

Danger Man: Austin Mini Cooper S

Jason King: Alfa Romeo 1750 GT Veloce

The Protectors: Citroën SM and Jensen Interceptor

The Persuaders: Aston Martin DBS and Ferrari Dino 246 GT

The Professionals: Mk III Ford Capri 3.0 S

The Avengers: Broadspeed Jaguar XJ12C

The Saint: Volvo P1800

The Sweeney: many brown Ford Cortinas, Granadas, Capris . . .

Ferrari GTOs

Ferrari only puts the 'GTO' badge on its most extreme road cars. In fact, it has made just three GTOs in its eighty-year history, including the new 599 GTO. How do the three classics compare?

GTO stands for Gran Turismo Omologato. *This is not a fancy Italian ice cream with sparklers in. It means a vehicle is:*

- *a high-performance luxury car designed for long-distance driving (a grand tourer)*

- *produced in limited numbers to meet the specific requirements of a race series (homologated).*

So a GTO is a rare, fast, powerful, comfortable car. And they're not bad-looking, either.

250 GTO

Thirty-nine produced between 1962 and 1964

- Engine 3L V12 (front-engined)
- Power 300hp
- Top speed 175mph

In 1962 the rules said manufacturers had to make 100 cars of the same model before that model was allowed to compete in the Group 3 Grand Touring Car racing. Ferrari numbered the 250 GTO with random numbers that made it look like they'd made more than 100, when they'd only made thirty-nine. Well done, Ferrari.

The 250 cost about £10,000 new, if Enzo Ferrari allowed you to buy it. Chris Evans paid £12 million for one in 2010.

'In the eyes of many, the **250 GTO** is the **greatest** car Ferrari ever produced. Certainly, it is the **greatest road racer** from the ultimate decade of road racing.'

288 GTO

272 produced between 1984-1987

🚗 Engine 2.9L V8 with twin turbos and fuel injection

💥 400hp

⏱ Top speed 189mph

By 1984 Ferrari had to make 200 cars to enter the new Group B Race series (with no cheating). But then the race series was abandoned, and the cars were never raced. It certainly looked racey, with the big front spoiler, four headlights and grilles in the bonnet.

'Because it has no racing pedigree, it's now **a bargain.** You could now **buy one** for as **little as . . . £400,000.'**

599 GTO

599 to be produced

🚗 Engine 6L V12

💥 Power 661hp

⏱ 0-62mph in 3.35s

⏱ Top speed 208mph

🏷 Cost £300,000

The 599 GTO is the street-legal version of the 599XX, which is the racing version of the 599 GTB (pay attention). It's the fastest, most powerful road car Ferrari has ever made. But Jeremy thought it was too hard to drive properly, while not being a proper race car. Fusspot.

'The speed! **THE SPEED!!** And **the noise** of the speed!'

'I don't feel I'm driving this car. I feel I'm just a **big lump of meat** that's **come along for the ride.'**

One Billion Cars . . .

Quite recently, they reckon the number of cars in the world passed one billion for the first time ever. That's a lot.

The car map of the world is changing. At the moment, almost one in every three cars in the world is in America. They made 7.8 million vehicles in 2009. Pretty impressive? Well, it used to be.

As countries get richer, they buy more cars. And who's getting richer, quickest? Yep, China. The Chinese made 18.3 million cars last year. The whole of Europe only made 16.9 million. Chinese cars may look mostly rubbish to us now – Jeremy and James found them pretty hilarious – but soon we may all be driving them.

So what about the exact numbers? Well, it's a bit tricky. Some countries aren't very efficient at registering new vehicles. Quite a few are rubbish at saying when a car has been scrapped. This map shows every country with more than 1% of the world's cars in 2002 (the **blue** bars) and what clever people think it will be in 2030 (the **red** bars).

Canada

United States

Mexico

Brazil

Chile

Argentina

All the other countries put together

100,000,000 cars

Cars per 100 population

Africa	3
Middle East	10
Far East	16
Central and South America	17
Eastern Europe	36
Western Europe	58
Pacific	56
Canada	62
America	83

and counting

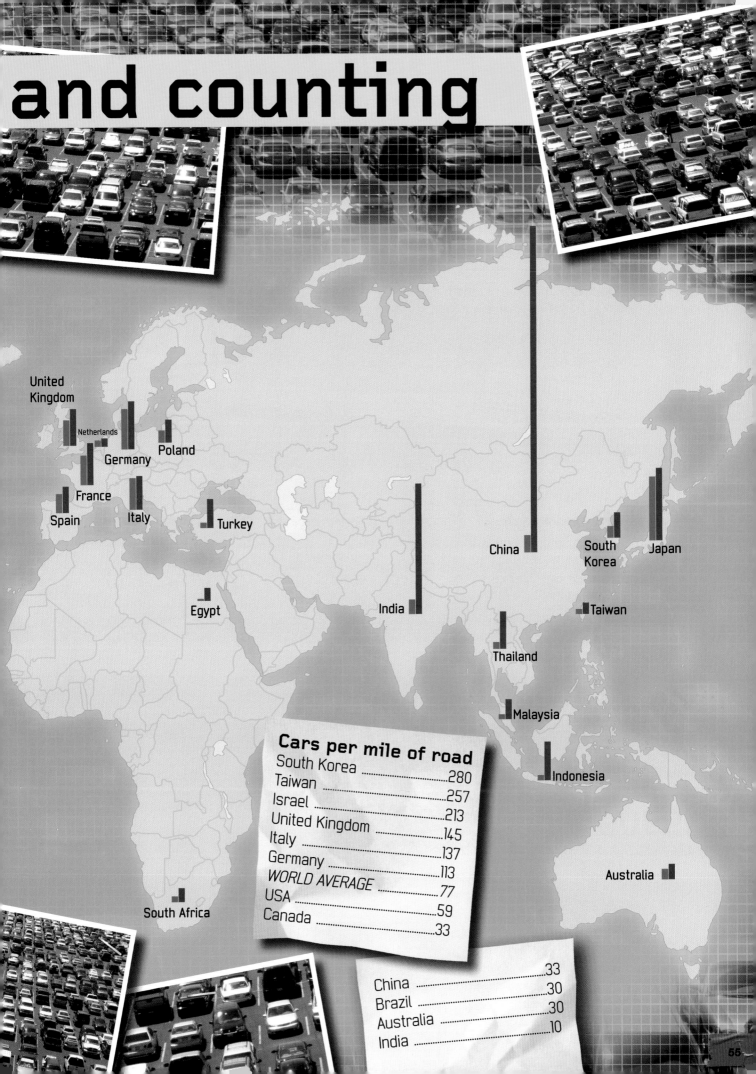

United Kingdom

Netherlands

Germany

Poland

France

Spain

Italy

Turkey

Egypt

India

China

South Korea

Japan

Taiwan

Thailand

Malaysia

Indonesia

Australia

South Africa

Cars per mile of road

South Korea	280
Taiwan	257
Israel	213
United Kingdom	145
Italy	137
Germany	113
WORLD AVERAGE	77
USA	59
Canada	33

China	33
Brazil	30
Australia	30
India	10

The Fastest Cars Ever

The Veyron Super Sport is the fastest car of the 2010s . . . so far. But what were the fastest cars of previous decades?

2010s

Bugatti Veyron Super Sport

267.9 mph

DISCLAIMER:
It's tricky to find out if historic speed tests were accurate and independent. Lamborghini, for example, claimed 190mph for the Countach in 1978, but no one else believed them.

2000s

SSC Ultimate Aero TT

256.2 mph

April 19, 2005
Bugatti Veyron – 253.8 mph

February 28, 2005
Koenigsegg CCR – 241 mph

1990s

McLaren F1

231 mph

Ferrari F40

1980s

202.7 mph

Porsche 959 – 197 mph

Ferrari 288 GTO – 188 mph

1970s

Lamborghini Countach LP400S

183 mph

1960s

174 mph

Lamborghini Miura P400 – 171 mph

Iso Rivolta Grifo A3/L 327 – 161 mph

Jaguar E-Type S1 3.8 – 151 mph

Ferrari 365 GTB/4 Daytona

1950s

140 mph

Jaguar XK120

1940s

124.6 mph

Mercedes-Benz 300SL

Join The Stig Fan Club

It's the craze that's not sweeping the nation! All you have to do is dress in white from head to toe, and never speak. Your parents may be really happy for you to join.

How to join

Complete the form below and send it, with fourteen gallons of unleaded biodiesel and a bag of supercar exhaust fumes, to the address on page 97.

What you get

- A membership card
- A selection of badges
- Stickers for your books and window
- A T-shirt with a picture on the front of a T-shirt
- A poster
- A life-size model of the Nürburgring (some assembly required)

Nürburgring

life-size model

Membership Form

Name . . . .
Address . . . .
Helmet size . . . .
Favourite flavour of custard . . . .
. . . .
. . . .
. . . .
. . . .
. . . .

Do you know what dogs are for?   YES/NO
Do you know which way is north?   YES/NO
I agree with the Terms and Conditions
of Membership below. ☐

Terms and Conditions of Membership

Some say these are the terms and conditions. Some say they're rather tedious. All we know is that they don't make any sense, and no one ever reads them. All right, you've read this far, but you're not going to make it to the end, are you? Of course not. They're far too boring. There may be some point to them if you're a lawyer, but not to anyone else. Who on earth takes any notice of the terms and conditions apart from the person who wrote them? That must be the most boring job in the world, writing terms and conditions. Or how about checking terms and conditions to see if there are any spelling mistakes in them? That's got to be pretty boring as well. These terms and conditions need something worthwhile in them, so here's a poem called *Desiderata*, written in 1927. Go placidly amidst the noise and haste, and remember what peace there may be in silence. As far as possible without surrender be on good terms with all persons. Speak your truth quietly and clearly; and listen to others, even the dull and the ignorant; they too have their story. Avoid loud and aggressive persons, they are vexations to the spirit. If you compare yourself with others, you may become vain or bitter; for always there will be greater and lesser persons than yourself. Enjoy your achievements as well as your plans. Keep interested in your own career, however humble; it is a real possession in the changing fortunes of time. Exercise caution in your business affairs; for the world is full of trickery. But let this not blind you to what virtue there is; many persons strive for high ideals; and everywhere life is full of heroism. Be yourself. Especially, do not feign affection. Neither be cynical about love; for in the face of all aridity and disenchantment it is as perennial as the grass. Take kindly the counsel of the years, gracefully surrendering the things of youth. Nurture strength of spirit to shield you in sudden misfortune. But do not distress yourself with dark imaginings. Many fears are born of fatigue and loneliness. Beyond a wholesome discipline, be gentle with yourself. You are a child of the universe, no less than the trees and the stars; you have a right to be here. And whether or not it is clear to you, no doubt the universe is unfolding as it should. Therefore be at peace with God, whatever you conceive Him to be, and whatever your labors and aspirations, in the noisy confusion of life keep peace with your soul. With all its sham, drudgery, and broken dreams, it is still a beautiful world. Be cheerful. Strive to be happy.

End Train Misery!

Fed up of being stuffed into a slow, crowded, expensive carriage full of stinky sweaty commuters? Wish there was a quicker, more private alternative with plenty of fresh air? Your wishes are answered! Say hello to the . . .

TGV-12 XJ-Spress Sports Train!!

'Even here we're stuck behind caravans!'

Benefits
- Only one carriage, with four racing seats
- Proper seatbelts (you'll need them)
- Much cheaper than boring old big trains
- Could be much faster than those slowcoaches
- Fantastic all-round views of the glorious British countryside
- Your own personal driver

Drawbacks
- Personal driver has strong opinions
- No protection from the weather . . .
- . . . or the flies, pebbles, bird poo, exhaust fumes and flames
- You won't be able to open your mouth, let alone talk
- Very noisy and extremely uncomfortable
- No food or drink available
- Speed is limited by whatever is in front of the XJ-S Sports Train

Answers

Page 10: Complete the Quote

BMW 1M:
'The 1M is like a **turkey curry on Boxing Day**.
It's made of leftovers'.

Eagle Speedster:
'It's spitting fire . . . it's a **Spitfire**! That's what it is!'

McLaren MP4-12C:
'You'd get more of a jolt if you drove a Rolls-Royce
over a **Jaffa Cake**'.

'The McLaren, then, is like a **pair of tights**. Very practical,
and very sensible'.

Ferrari 599 GTO:
'This is not a car, it's a **wild animal**'.

Range Rover Evoque:
'Lovely, lovely tarmac. It's like a **cool hand passed across
your fevered brow**'.

Jaguar XKR-S:
'It feels and sounds as if it's being fuelled by a mixture of
plutonium and **wild animals**'.

James:
'Everyone should own a **Mini** at some point or you are
incomplete as a human being!'

Marauder:
'It's like off-roading quite a **large building**!'

Page 20: James' Orienteering Challenge

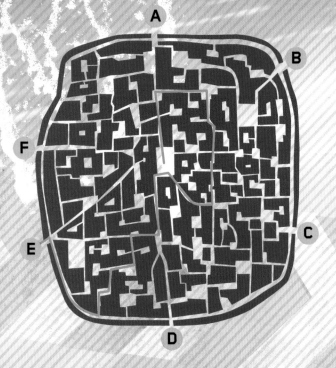

Page 21: Modern Classics

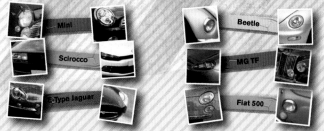

Page 40: Build the perfect *Top Gear* Car!

James: Fiat Panda, Ferrari F430, Porsche Boxster S, Rolls-Royce Corniche.

Richard: Land Rover Defender, Porsche 911, Dodge Challenger, Morgan Aeromax.

Jeremy: Citroën DS3 Racing, Maserati Quattroporte, Skoda Yeti, Mercedes SLR McLaren.

Page 42: Electric Car Charging Maze

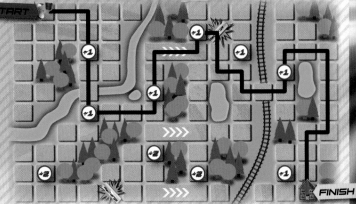

Page 45: That is the Sound of . . . POWER!

1) Car Darts, *2)* Airship Caravan, *3)* Reliant Rocket,
4) Mini Ski jump, *5)* Toyboata, *6)* Caravan Conkers,
7) Toyota on a Towerblock, *8)* Reliant Robin

Page 46: Supercars from Around the World

Hulme F1 Champion 1967: New Zealand

Beck LM 800: Switzerland

Marussia B2: Russia

Genty Akylone: France

Rossin-Bertin Vorax: Brazil

De Veno Arrinera: Poland

HTT Pléthore LC-750: Canada

Fisker Karma: Finland

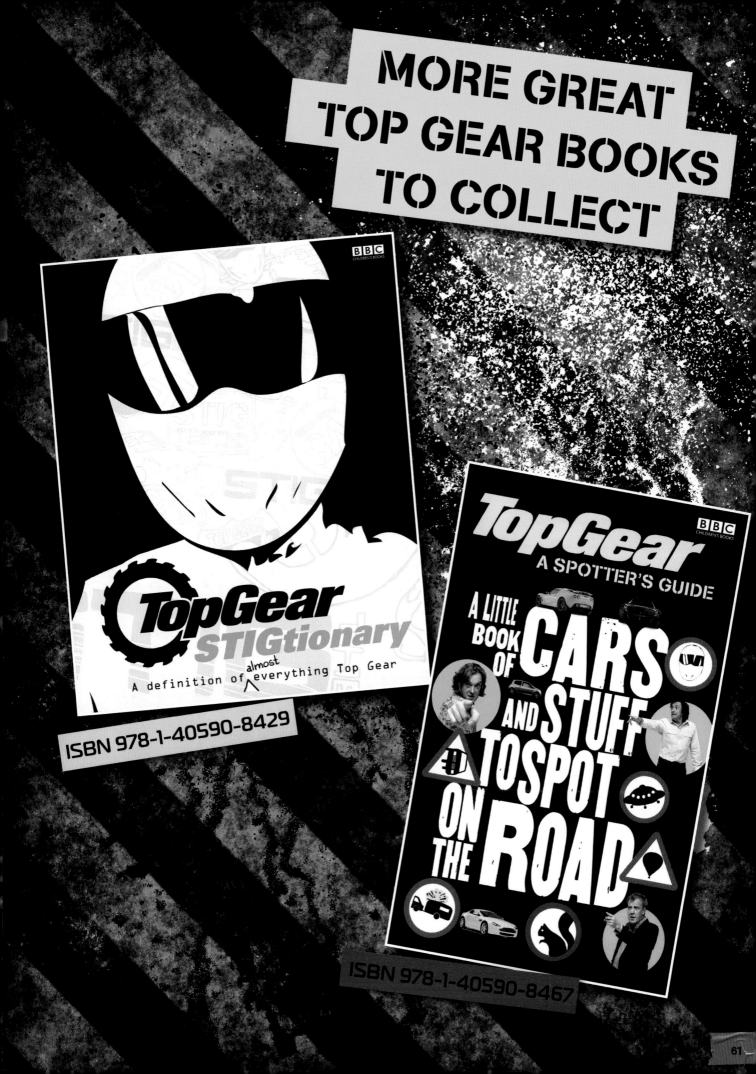